STOP
YOUR FEAR
BEFORE IT STOPS YOU

Fatai Kasali

Stop Your Fear Before It Stops You © 2018 Fatai Kasali.

The author has asserted his right to be identified as the author of this work in accordance with the Copyright, Designs and Patents Act 1988.

All rights reserved. No part of this publication may be reproduced, stored in a retrieval system, or transmitted, in any form or by any means, electronic, mechanical, photocopying, recording or otherwise without the prior permission of the author.

Scripture quotations from The Authorised (King James) Version. Rights in the Authorized Version in the United Kingdom are vested in the Crown. Reproduced by permission of the Crown's patentee, Cambridge University Press.

Published in the United Kingdom by Glory Publishing.

ISBN: 978-1-9996849-5-2

Acknowledgments

To God be the glory for the grace to write this book. I give God all the praise and adoration for giving me the inspiration through His Spirit. This has made possible the writing of this book.

My wife, Felicia Ebunlomo, gave me priceless support during the writing of this book. My two sons, Daniel and David, have been very supportive.

To all those who have contributed one way or the other to the beauty of this work, thank you very much. May God Almighty bless you all.

Introduction

For God hath not given us the spirit of fear;
but of power, and of love, and of a sound mind.

2 TIMOTHY 1:7

If fear is not from God, then it is very likely to originate from the devil, our adversary.

Fear has been defined as fake evidence appearing real. This means that fear is the expectation of an evil occurrence or danger that almost never materialises in the way that is expected. It is about imagined evil. Fear sets into motion; a series of terrifying possibilities within the mind of its victim that produce a painful emotion. The victim of fear never rests, for his mind is preoccupied with frightening thoughts that are simply fictitious.

This book explores a variety of ways in which fear can stop a person from properly functioning as the person God created him to be. You will discover fear as a stopper and how it attempts to stop people. It is very possible that after you have read this book, you will realise how fear has been stopping you in many situations. You may discover how fear has destroyed your vision, halted your dreams and prevented you from taking part in endeavours you enjoyed in the past. Fear is a terminator, able to terminate a journey that was supposed to lead a person to his promised land. Fear can suffocate a good project until it dies. Fear is a stopper.

But take heart! Fear may be a stopper, but this book will show you how to stop fear itself. Through this book; you will develop an understanding of what strategies to employ in order to stop things that make you afraid.

The story of David versus Goliath is used in this book as a case study to explore how to stop fear. You will learn how David confronted the fear of Goliath and defeated it – using a single, ordinary stone. For many days Goliath silenced the whole nation of Israel due to fear. But a young man named David came forward to challenge the same Goliath who the people of Israel considered undefeatable. There is nothing making you afraid that you cannot defeat! Faith is stronger than fear.

This book will teach you how to take steps of faith to stop and defeat your fear. If David could do it, you also can do it.

It is my prayer that after you finish reading this book, your faith will grow stronger and enable you to overcome your fear and start living a life controlled by faith, not fear. God bless you.

Contents

1. Types of fear 9
2. Operations of the spirit of fear 15
3. Open doors to fear 21
4. Fear is a stopper 37
5. How to stop your fear 51
6. Fear not 81

Chapter 1

TYPES OF FEAR

─────■─────

There are two types of fear: godly and ungodly fear.

Godly fear is a reverential fear that we show to our God. It is godly fear that makes us relate to God with respect and honour, without disobedience.

Ungodly fear is a painful emotion that originates from expectation of evil or danger. It comes with anxiety and leads to enslavement. This kind of fear is demonic.

EXAMPLES OF UNGODLY FEAR INCLUDE:

1. **Fear of men**: this fear makes you treat people you are afraid of differently to others – you will always want to please them, even if it involves doing something wrong.

2. **Fear of the unknown**: this generates insecurity about your future. If it takes root in your life, it drives you to make a series of ungodly efforts to protect your future. You may commit the sin of covetousness in the attempt to secure your future.

3. **Fear of danger**: this kind of fear makes you avoid any situation capable of exposing you to danger or risk. It prevents you from taking risks in life, even when the potential benefits are great.

4. **Fear of condemnation**: this is a fear that arises when a fault is committed. You hide or lie when you make a mistake or do something wrong, because of the fear of being rebuked or

condemned. There is no boldness to tell the truth and apologise for the error committed, in order to shame the devil.

5. **Fear of failure**: this is the fear that makes you avoid trying new things because you don't want to fail. If you have failed in certain things in the past, when you attempt to try them again, the devil will remind you of your past failures and this will put fear in you. You stop trying again because you don't want to fail again.

6. **Fear of battle**: this kind of fear usually comes when you are fighting against stronger enemies. This can make you accept defeat even before the battle begins. You surrender and accept defeat because you believe you can't defeat your enemies.

7. **Fear of exposure**: this kind of fear comes when somebody in your life holds certain secrets about you. This can make you pay excessive attention or offer unjustified respect to the person who knows your secret. You turn the person into an idol because you are afraid of him or her exposing your secret, and you become vulnerable to their manipulation.

8. **Fear of other gods**: this kind of fear makes you afraid of people who have supernatural powers such as witches, witchdoctors, shamans or wiccans. This fear can deceive some people into forming alliances with agents of darkness as a way of appeasing them. They decide to reconcile with witches and other people with demonic access because they are afraid of their powers.

9. **Fear of death**: this kind of fear hinders people from taking any risks, rising to any challenges or confronting any dangers because of the fear of death. They live a restricted life and have no achievements. History has shown that those who fear death never live long. The fear of death kills them prematurely.

10. **Fear of pain**: this kind of fear makes you avoid any exercise that involves physical or emotional pain. If you are afraid of pain you will always seek the easy route in whatever you

do, and you will avoid any task that causes pain, despite the benefits. People that fear pain don't pursue big dreams.

11. **Fear of change**: this kind of fear makes you prefer the old to the new, regardless of the potential of new things. It makes you see evil or wrong in the new. You think new things may fail you, so, it's safest to stick with the old. You are afraid of the uncertainty that comes with anything new.

12. **Fear of lack**: this makes you hoard good things and avoid spending. Those that fear lack are usually stingy and not generous.

13. **Fear of exploitation**: this kind of fear prevents you from entering into any partnership with people because you are afraid that they may exploit you. You don't like to engage in business with people due to fear that they may use you for their own advantage.

14. **Fear of abandonment**: this makes you avoid forming relationships with people because you are afraid of being abandoned someday. This fear makes you prefer being lonely than being in a relationship that might break down at any time. This fear prevents many people from getting married because they consider it more terrible to be divorced than never to marry at all.

15. **Fear of loneliness**: this kind of fear makes you stay in a relationship despite the fact that you are not happy in it. This is because you are afraid of being alone. The fear then makes you stay in a toxic relationship because you think it is better than being alone. This fear makes you always want to please your partner because you don't want him or her to leave you.

16. **Fear of intimacy**: this kind of fear makes you avoid close relationships because you don't want people to know your secrets. You are afraid of intimacy because you think that it will give people access to certain secrets of your life, and this will make you vulnerable. Consequently, you prefer casual and shallow friendships.

17. **Fear of the crowd**: this fear makes you avoid anything that will make you face the public. This is because you are afraid of what the crowd may think about your appearance or performance.

18. **Fear of loss**: this makes you over-protective about whatever you have. You do whatever possible to keep your possessions. You find it difficult to let go in life. For example, if you are afraid of losing your job, you will over-protect it by, for example, tolerating every negative aspect of it or being antagonistic to those who might threaten it.

19. **Fear of decision-making**: this kind of fear comes in because you are afraid of the possible consequences of your decision. This makes you give excuses for your inaction on decisions. You are over-conscious of the possible challenges and exposure that a decision may bring to you.

20. **Fear of status**: this kind of fear creates in you; a low self-esteem due to your low status. You believe that you are not fit for certain responsibilities because of your low status in life. For example, you may think that people will not accept you as their leader because you are not as well-educated as them, or have a lower grade job.

21. **Fear of offence**: this makes you avoid any situation that might cause you to offend people or people to offend you. Because you don't want to offend others, you may choose not to offer them certain advice. Similarly, because you don't want people to offend you, you may limit your relationships with them. It is all about fear.

22. **Fear of rejection**: this prevents you from applying for certain opportunities because you are afraid of being rejected. It blinds you to the possibility of acceptance in whatever you do. It hinders you from contesting for a position even if you are very qualified.

23. **Needless or unexplainable fear**: this is the kind of fear that you cannot offer any credible or plausible reason for. You are unable to explain what is making you afraid. It is irrational fear.

TYPES OF FEAR

PHOBIAS

These are different kinds of severe and unreasonable fears that have been observed by psychologists. Phobias are a form of anxiety disorder and are characterised by intense and irrational fears of an object or situation that poses no real threat. Examples of fears described as common phobias include the following:

Acrophobia: The fear of *height*.

Agoraphobia: The fear of *open and public places*.

Aichmophobia: The fear of *sharp objects*.

Algophobia: The fear of *pain*.

Anthropophobia: The fear of *man or a particular person*.

Astraphobia: The fear of *thunder, lightning or storms*.

Claustrophobia: A fear of *closed places*.

Ereuthophobia: Fear of *blushing*.

Gynephobia: Fear of *women or a particular woman*.

Haemophobia: Fear of *blood*.

Hydrophobia: Fear of *water*.

Monophobia: Fear of *solitude*.

Necrophobia: Fear of *dead bodies*.

Nyctophobia: Fear of *darkness*.

Ochlophobia: Fear of *crowds*.

Pathophobia: Fear of *disease*.

Pyrophobia: Fear of *fire*.

Thanatophobia: Fear of death.

Toxiphobia: Fear of poisons.

Zoophobia: Fear of animals.

There are numerous manifestations of this tormenting, binding, ensnaring fear apparent in our world today. Multitudes of people fear for their safety, hiding behind closed doors and barred windows, some even arming themselves with lethal weapons.

Chapter 2

OPERATIONS OF THE SPIRIT OF FEAR

It is important for you to understand how fear influences your daily life activities. Fear is a spirit and it influences the daily life of its victims. We shall examine how fear operates in a victim. This understanding will help you to detect when you are in the grip of fear. With this knowledge, you can then take practical steps to resist it.

1. Whatever you are afraid of will torment you.

Fear causes pain, be it emotional or psychological. It makes you exhibit negative emotions. It makes you suffer unnecessarily. Therefore fear is an affliction from the devil.

2. Whatever you are afraid of is more likely to happen to you.

Fear is a spirit which operates through the circumstances of life. For example, if you don't invest your money for fear of losing it, you will lose out on the potential returns of investment, and it will devalue over time, so resulting in loss. This is because when your actions are controlled by fear, not by wisdom, they lead you into loss.

3. Whatever you are afraid of will control you.

It will control your imagination, thoughts, words, actions, expectations, plans and dreams. For example, if you are afraid of change, you will always prefer the old to the new. This fear will make you act favourably towards the old, even when something new is better. Fear therefore controls you, not wisdom.

4. Whatever you are afraid of will pervert your view.

Fear will stop you seeing the situation in the correct way, in the way that reflects reality. You will tend to exaggerate things you are afraid of.

5. Whatever you are afraid of will suppress and oppress you continually.

If not defeated, fear does not give breathing space to its victims. Fear is able to sustain its attack on your mind indefinitely, unless you defeat it.

6. Whatever you are afraid of will follow you around.

For example, if you are afraid of death, you will always see death wherever you go. Even when you run away from certain death, you will still see death in the new place you run to. It follows you around until you send it packing from your life. Because it is a spirit, fear is not localised. Your fear will not go because of your change of location. If you pack out of a location because you afraid of your neighbour, in your new location, the same spirit of fear will discover another neighbour or person you will be afraid of.

7. Whatever you are afraid of will expand its territory in your life.

Fear expands its territory when it is allowed to operate without check. For example, if you fear your manager at work, soon, you will begin to fear the deputy manager and later the assistant deputy manager, then the secretary and eventually, all your colleagues. If you still fail to confront your fear, it will continue to rule over you until it reduces you to nothing.

8. Whatever you are afraid of will never leave you unless you confront it.

Fear does not go voluntarily; it must be driven away. James 4:7 says we must resist the devil and then he will flee from us.

9. Whatever you are afraid of will make you childish.

Your fear will make you behave like a child. You can't think in a mature way concerning whatever makes you afraid. If you are afraid of heights, you will always think and act poorly when it comes to anything that has to do with height. Therefore, if you want to discover the type of fear you have, find out about the thing that makes you act or think immaturely.

10. Whatever you are afraid of will become your focus.

Fear attracts attention. What makes you afraid will always attract your attention. Unfortunately, whatever fear has become your focus will always appear bigger than its real size. For example, you are likely to exaggerate the strength of a man that you are afraid of. The man will always become your focus.

11. Whatever you are afraid of will become your confession.

For example, if you are afraid of failure you are likely to always be confessing failure concerning your endeavour. If you think fear, you will speak fear. Therefore, take notice of your negative speech; it could be a reflection of your fear.

12. Whatever you are afraid of will make you run when nobody is chasing you.

Fear keeps you alert to the thing you fear; you will see it where it does not exist. It is your imagination.

13. Whatever you are afraid of will become your boundary.

Fear makes itself a 'no go' area of your life. If you are afraid of travelling by aeroplane, flying will become a no go area for you. Fear brings negative censors. It dictates your endeavour and encounters. Therefore, things you consider a no go area in your life could be a reflection of your fear.

14. Whatever you are afraid of will steal your peace.

For example, you are likely to become restless when you are asked to appear before a crowd, if you have a fear of crowds. To understand your fears, check things that make you anxious and worried.

15. Whatever you are afraid of will control your life aspirations.

For example, you may not become a doctor because of your fear of blood. Therefore it is important for you to check what makes you like what you like and what makes you hate what you hate. It could be due to fear and not what God has told you.

16. Whatever you are afraid of will drain your energy.

Things you are afraid of will consume your strength. No matter how courageous you appear to be, when you reach the territory of your fear, all your confidence will disappear. Therefore, be mindful of things that make you weak and powerless; it could be an indication of your fear.

17. Whatever you afraid of will split your mind.

Fear promotes double-mindedness. It is difficult to exhibit genuine faith in God with a divided mind controlled by fears. Faith and fear can't co-exist in the same place; one has to give place to the other. For example, it may be true that one part of your mind is telling you to enter into a certain relationship, but your fear of rejection will make you unwilling to do so. The mind is divided.

18. Whatever you are afraid of will hinder your health.

The connection between mind and body is not fully understood, but it is beyond doubt that there are psychosomatic illnesses – diseases of the body caused by problems of the mind. For example, stress is known to have an indirect impact on heart health. Fear can influence a series of sicknesses. It may affect your blood pressure and temperature. If you notice a persistent headache or another irregularity within your body, it may be an indication that your fear is dominating your thoughts and imagination.

19. Whatever you are afraid of will become your obsession.

Fears have a habit of continually intruding into our thoughts. Even when you don't want to think about it, what you are afraid of will surface in your thoughts. If you fear something, ideas will continually crop up in your thoughts about how to avoid or escape whatever is making you afraid. You can't stop thinking about it. That is an obsession. That is your fear. It needs dealing with.

20. Whatever you are afraid of makes you feel helpless.

Things that you believe you can't deal with; lead you to fear. Your fear is usually a product of your belief in your helplessness. For example, when you think that you don't have what it takes to handle situations in a relationship, you become afraid of entering into a relationship. Check your feelings of helplessness as they will help you to identify your fears.

21. Whatever you are afraid of will attempt to diminish your God in your heart.

Fear makes you question God's faithfulness. Fear is an enemy of faith in God. The more you yield to your fear, the more you will lose focus on God and the more you will move away from faith. Fear prevents you from seeing God in your situation. For example, if you are afraid of the future, you won't trust God for your future, and if you don't believe God is in charge of your future, you will be afraid.

22. Whatever you are afraid of makes you a prophet of doom to yourself.

Fear makes you believe that harm will come to you if you take a certain course of action. For example, if you are afraid of flying and you face a situation where you need to travel by air, you may start having a dream of a plane crash or believing that your plane will crash. Or if you fear financial losses, you may start believing that your business will collapse or you will lose your job, or even prophesy it. If this is so, it is the spirit of fear that is giving you revelation and prophecy of evil, not the Spirt of God. The spirit of fear is trying to frighten you so that your choices will be totally controlled by it. Therefore, you may need to examine the words you have spoken or the negative beliefs you have held about yourself, in order to detect if the spirit of fear is at work in you. Then ask the Lord to set you free, because *"God hath not given us the spirit of fear; but of power, and of love, and of a sound mind"* (2 Timothy 1:7).

Chapter 3

OPEN DOORS TO FEAR

The question you will need to ask yourself is: why am I afraid? Truly the devil is an agent of fear, but there are certain conducive situations that must exist in your life before he can gain access to attack you with fear.

In this chapter, we will examine various avenues that create opportunities for the spirit of fear to enter our lives.

1. Sin

Sin is every act of unrighteousness and breaking of the law of God.

> *The wicked flee when no man pursueth: but the righteous are bold as a lion.* PROVERBS 28:1.

'The wicked' are sinners that are habitually unrighteous. The devil is the author of sin and fear. When he tempts people into committing sin, he gains access into their lives to steal their peace and make them live in fear. If you notice persistent fear in your mind, you will need to check your lifestyle. Sin invites fear. Sin makes you develop an evil imagination. People that practise sins have a strong tendency to imagine that evil things will befall them. It is impossible to be genuinely fearless when you know that you practise evil, because evil has consequences that are to be feared. They may not always materialise in this life, but the fear of them builds up nonetheless.

2. Guilt

This is a painful emotion experienced by people who believe they have done wrong. Guilt then creates an imagination of possible evil occurrences as a punishment for the evil they believe they have committed.

> *And the messengers returned to Jacob, saying, We came to thy brother Esau, and also he cometh to meet thee, and four hundred men with him. Then Jacob was greatly afraid and distressed...*
> GENESIS 32:6-7

In this story, Jacob was greatly afraid to meet his brother, Esau, because of the guilt he carried for stealing the blessings of Esau in the past. A guilty conscience can make you see danger where there is no danger, and thereby makes you afraid.

3. Doubt

When you start doubting the faithfulness of God, the devil will attack your mind with a series of wrong thoughts that will put you under fear.

> *A double minded man is unstable in all his ways.* JAMES 1:8

A man of double mind is unstable in thoughts, decisions, loyalties and imagination. He is neither here nor there. When your mind is divided, it becomes easy for the devil to put deception into your mind, by creating a wrong thought about something. Therefore, if you don't want to live under fear, believe whatever God tells you or promises you and stand by it.

4. Ignorance of the promises of God

When you don't know God's promises regarding certain issues of your life, you will live in fear because the devil will bring you lies.

For example, if you don't know that God has made provision for your healing, you will be afraid of sickness instead of declaring God's promises over it. Similarly, if you don't know that God has made you more than a conqueror, you will be afraid of the enemy instead of declaring to the enemy that you are more than a conqueror and can't be defeated.

> *My people are destroyed for lack of knowledge: because thou hast rejected knowledge, I will also reject thee, that thou shalt be no priest to me: seeing thou hast forgotten the law of thy God, I will also forget thy children.* HOSEA 4:6

The knowledge is available but people choose not to learn it. If you don't learn the promises of God concerning your problem, the devil will blow it out of all proportion in your heart to make you afraid.

5. Childishness

To be childish means to refuse to mature. A ten-year-old child will definitely be afraid of challenges that are meant for a man who is 40. Therefore, if at 40 years of age your maturity is still at the stage of a ten-year-old, then when you face adult challenges, you will come under fear.

> *When I was a child, I spake as a child, I understood as a child, I thought as a child: but when I became a man, I put away childish things.* 1 CORINTHIANS 13:11

The childish things are the imperfect conceptions and reasoning of a child. Your fear could be due to the way you think about the situation. If you think in a shallow way, the devil will take advantage of it to show you a picture of that situation that is not real. Deep thinking with a matured mind gives you understanding about your situation, which takes away undue fear.

6. Negative attention

This refers to too much attention and analysis of a problem. When you focus excessively on a problem, it will gradually take your attention from Jesus.

> *But when he saw the wind boisterous, he was afraid; and beginning to sink, he cried, saying, Lord, save me.* MATTHEW 14:30

This verse comes from the story of Peter walking on water without fear – until he started focusing on the wind instead of Jesus. When you focus on your problem, the devil will expand it in your sight and imagination. This creates fear in your heart. Instead of focusing on your problem, it is better to focus on Jesus who is able to help you. That doesn't mean you ignore the problem, but you don't let it dominate your thinking.

7. Confession

Your confession indicates your agreement and belief. If you confess negative things, this allows the devil to work on your heart. If you are continually confessing evil, you open the door to him to bring the same evil into your imagination, and very soon, the evil will appear more real to you than the good. The evil you confess then captures more of your thoughts and expectations, and fear creeps into your life through the devil's manipulation.

> *And all the congregation lifted up their voice, and cried; and the people wept that night.* NUMBERS 14:1

The people of Israel started crying and weeping because they were seeing death in their thoughts and imagination. How did they reach this stage? Since the beginning of their journey from Egypt, they had been confessing death. Whenever they came across any new challenge, they started confessing that they were going to die.

Therefore, death appeared more real to them than life, and they believed their own 'propaganda'. The possibility of death became a probability and then a certainty, in their minds. It made them so afraid that they started crying, out of self-pity.

8. Obsession

This is a situation where a person's thoughts or feelings are persistently dominated by a certain idea or desire or imagination. It means that your thoughts and feelings have been taken over by things that occupy them. Unfortunately, if your obsession is on something that is negative, fear becomes inevitable. For example, if the thought of being found guilty in a court hearing dominates your thoughts, you will become afraid of the hearing day, though, it has not even come. Similarly, if you become obsessed about the manager at work who hates you, you will soon be afraid of him because you will begin to imagine all the terrible things he might do.

> *Let the words of my mouth, and the meditation of my heart, be acceptable in thy sight, O LORD, my strength, and my redeemer.*
> PSALMS 19:14

Meditation is the process of concentrating on certain words or ideas. If you are continually thinking about something negative, you get obsessed with it, and it opens the door for the devil to manipulate your perception of it. The devil will attempt to call good evil and evil good. You are on a journey towards being afraid of what is not real.

9. Idolatory

> *Little children, keep yourselves from idols. Amen.* 1 JOHN 5:21

An idol is anything that replaces God in your heart. Whatever occupies more space in your heart than God has become your idol.

Whatever you love above God is your idol. It is only a matter of time before that idol will lead you astray from God. The devil is the founder of idols. He will always encourage people to stop giving worship to God and instead worship himself.

Whatever you idolise will receive your worship. The pay cheque from the devil for accepting an idol is fear. It is only when your heart is totally occupied by the love of God that you will operate your life with a sense of genuine security. An idol takes your worship from God, so it can take you away from a sense of divine security. The consequence of idolatry is many kinds of fear.

10. Troubled heart

> *And when Zacharias saw him, he was troubled, and fear fell upon him.*
> LUKE 1:12

A troubled heart is a heart that is agitated and unstable due to a lot of concerns. It has no resting place; it cannot settle. It is filled with a series of uncertainties. When the devil sees such a heart, he comes in to lie to it and create even more confusion. Fear then sets in.

11. Failure to forgive yourself

It is one thing for you to be forgiven by somebody else; it is quite another for you to forgive yourself. When you fail to forgive yourself for whatever sin you committed, you create an opportunity for the devil to attack your mind with guilt and make you feel you deserve to be punished. This can persist even if you know scriptures like Romans 8:1 which says there is no condemnation in Christ Jesus.

> *And his brethren also went and fell down before his face; and they said, Behold, we be thy servants. And Joseph said unto them, Fear not: for am I in the place of God?* GENESIS 50:18-19

Due to lack of self-forgiveness, Joseph's brothers were under the fear of expectation of punishment by Joseph due to the evil they did to him many years previously. Truly; Joseph had forgiven them, but they had not forgiven themselves. This started creating in them; the fear of retribution from Joseph. If you fail to forgive yourself for any wrongdoing, the devil will work on your guilt and make you fear a future punishment for your sin or a bad consequence of it. Your heart will forever be haunted by your past wrongdoings, so, you need to not just receive God's forgiveness but be able to forgive yourself too.

12. Memory of a past failure

If you have failed in some endeavours in the past and want to correct that by doing it rightly in the future, your memory of failure is almost bound to resurface. Some people can use that to fire their determination to succeed this time, but for others, the memory can become a deterrent to future success. And then, the more you give in to that fear, the bigger it becomes and the more you will be afraid to attempt the same thing again. The longer you yield to this fear of repeating a failure, the more the devil will make it more real and it will plague your imagination. This may eventually force you to abandon the idea of succeeding where you had failed.

> *Now when he had left speaking, he said unto Simon, Launch out into the deep, and let down your nets for a draught. And Simon answering said unto him, Master, we have toiled all the night, and have taken nothing: nevertheless at thy word I will let down the net.* LUKE 5:4-5

In this story, when Jesus told Peter to spread his nets into the waters where they had caught nothing previously, the memory of past failure came alive within Peter. There was a possibility that fear of repeating that failure would prevent Peter from obeying Jesus' instruction, but fortunately Peter's trust in Jesus overcame his fears and he reaped the benefit with a big catch of fish.

If you have failed in a certain business before, then the fear of losing your money again will no doubt raise its head when you want to invest in the same business or a similar venture again. But if there is good reason to believe that it will work this time, you shouldn't let the devil manipulate your fears and prevent you from having another try. Many people have been unable to follow the philosophy, "If at first you don't succeed, try, try again," because of fear of repeating a failure.

13. Lovelessness

> *There is no fear in love; but perfect love casteth out fear: because fear hath torment. He that feareth is not made perfect in love.*
> 1 JOHN 4:18

Conversely, this verse indicates that where there is no love, there is fear. The person you hate will always make you afraid. It is unlikely that you will feel comfortable letting the person you hate prepare food for you to eat. Even if the person has no intention of poisoning you, the devil will convince you that he has.

Hatred creates an opportunity for the devil to manipulate people's reasoning. When you don't walk in love with people, you will be uncomfortable with them. The people you don't show love to will always appear like your enemies, even if they are not. It is love that casts out fear. This is the reason why the devil likes breeding enmity between people, because it will create an opportunity for him to control them; using the weapon of fear. Whenever you discover that you are afraid of certain people, check your love towards them.

14. Carnality

> *For to be carnally minded is death; but to be spiritually minded is life and peace.* ROMANS 8:6

Carnality brings a person under the dominion of the fleshly impulses of the body. Such a person lives to please his human desires – for pleasures like food, sex, status, wealth and comfort. His mind functions outside the law of God. Such a mind can never have rest because genuine rest is only found under the control of the Spirit of God. A carnal mind never has enough, so it can't rest, as it's always seeking more or something better. It is never satisfied. It is in a race it will never win.

Carnality's ambitions are created by the fear of not having enough, or not appearing to have enough in the eyes of others, or losing what you have, and its struggles are to overcome its self-created fear. If you want to avoid being under the torment of fear, avoid carnality.

15. Evil report

Evil reports or words from others include every sort of negative statement that has its origin in doubting God's faithfulness. The purpose of every evil report is to make you expect that a particular 'fate' will happen to you. When you accept and believe an evil report, the consequence is fear that it will come true. It is generally impossible for somebody to receive a prediction that he will die tomorrow and for that person to still be at peace within himself.

> *Whither shall we go up? Our brethren have discouraged our heart, saying, The people is greater and taller than we; the cities are great and walled up to heaven; and moreover we have seen the sons of the Anakims there.* DEUTERONOMY 1:28

The majority of the Israelites lost their courage in the wilderness (desert) because they accepted and believed the evil report brought back to them by ten spies they had sent to spy on the land they planned to invade. But the people who did not accept or believe this negative report showed courage. Many people have died before their time not because of the evil report they received, but the fear of its fulfilment. So if you don't want your life to be controlled by evil reports, you will need to disapprove and disbelieve them. Trust instead in what God's Word says about your situation.

16. Wrong exposure

If you are constantly exposing yourself to demonised materials, you will increase the probability of the demons behind such materials entering your life and starting to torment you. For example, there are people who pick up the spirit of fear when watching horror films. When the demon that sponsored such a film gains access into the lives of those who watched, that demon will start creating fears within them, using the memory of the pictures and sound from the films they watched. If this demon is not evicted the fears will grow within the person and spiritual bondage may result.

> *Wherefore come out from among them, and be ye separate, saith the Lord, and touch not the unclean thing; and I will receive you.*
> 2 CORINTHIANS 6:17

This Bible verse tells us not to touch any unclean thing. This is because when we interact with unclean things, we come into contact with the demon acting behind it, which can be the start of a terrible battle with the demonic in our lives.

17. Abuse

Abuse includes any form of maltreatment. When a person suffers abuse from a fellow human being, it may allow a spirit of fear to take hold of their life. For example, a lady who has suffered abuse from a man during a relationship may develop a wrong impression of men in general, which may permit the spirit of fear to enter her life. This spirit of fear will then make her always afraid of entering into another relationship with any man.

In Exodus 2, the Israelites were abused for many years by the

Pharaoh. The fear that then grew in their hearts was not only towards Pharaoh but every Egyptian around them. In the same way, a person who suffers abuse from one man from a certain race or country may become afraid of every person from that race or country, thinking that they are all the same. The spirit of fear may be behind such a general negative conclusion.

18. Wrong teaching

If you have been wrongly taught about certain facts in life, this may open a door to the entrance of the spirit of fear into your life. There are teachings, taboos and traditions that promote unbelief and fear. For example, in some cultures pregnant women are told not to walk outside when it's raining. This kind of superstition makes every pregnant woman who believes such teaching afraid of the rain, and any who are caught in a rain shower will then be afraid of what will happen. That is why it is wise to check what is actually making you afraid and if it has a spiritual basis or is just a rational fear.

> *Then came to Jesus scribes and Pharisees, which were of Jerusalem, saying, Why do thy disciples transgress the tradition of the elders? For they wash not their hands when they eat bread.*
> MATTHEW 15:1-2

The context of this story is that; the Israelites were taught, in accordance with the Law of Moses, that people must wash their hands before eating food because doing otherwise would made them unclean. But here Jesus debunked such teaching because washing your hands has no relevance to spiritual purity (though it's a wise thing to do for reasons of hygiene, of course, and that may be why God gave this teaching to Moses). Unfortunately, those who hold on to such teachings will come under guilt and fear if they find themselves accidentally breaking the teaching. In order to be free from the dominion of the spirit of fear, you may need to unlearn certain wrong things you have been taught.

19. Lack of preparation

When you are about to face a situation you did not properly prepare for, the devil will attempt to attack your mind with fear of the possible consequences. For example, if you fail to prepare for old age, when you are approaching the end of your working life, the devil may attack your mind with fears about the vulnerability that comes with old age. Similarly, an examination you did not prepare for is likely to make you afraid of failure when it is approaching. The battle you did not prepare for will make you afraid.

> *Go to the ant, thou sluggard; consider her ways, and be wise: which having no guide, overseer, or ruler, provideth her meat in the summer, and gathereth her food in the harvest.* PROVERBS 6:6-8

Many ants hoard up their food in the summer so they will not be hungry in winter. What you prepare for will not be able to make you afraid.

20. Lack of gratitude

To show gratitude is to be appreciative of what you have received from another person and God. This will only be possible if you focus on what you have instead of what you don't have. Excessive focus on your needs will shift your focus away from the other things God has blessed you with. You will be thinking and talking about your needs as if you had nothing else. Fear of being unable to obtain what you don't have will soon consume you, and you will start imagining terrible scenarios that are unrealistic.

But when you show gratitude to God for what He has given you, your trust in God's provision will rise within you. This dispels fear. An ungrateful heart will never be free from fear.

> *But now our soul is dried away: there is nothing at all, beside this manna, before our eyes.* NUMBERS 11:6

In this verse, Israel shows no appreciation to God for giving them manna to eat but instead the people are consumed with what they do not have. This made them undervalue the food they had and magnify what they desired. They were constantly dissatisfied and lived in hopelessness of ever obtaining their so-called needs. They became restless. An ungrateful heart will never have hope. So if you don't want to be captured by the spirit of fear, you will need to be grateful for what you have.

21. Indecision

> *A double minded man is unstable in all his ways.* JAMES 1:8

When you find it difficult to make up your mind on an issue, your mind is not at rest. In such a situation of restlessness of the mind, you are open to the devil's deceptions. He will attempt to exploit your distraction, to lie to you, giving you fake possibilities. This is the reason why you will notice that the longer you are undecided, the harder it becomes to make a decision. The devil will start attacking your mind with a series of options, most probably making you afraid of complications. You then become afraid of taking a decision, in case you get it wrong.

There are many people who find it difficult to make up their minds on an issue due to fear of making a mistake. Every option that comes to their mind comes with a fear of possible complications or failure. But you must understand that every decision has its own consequences, both negative and positive. If you are afraid of the possible negative consequences, you will never be able to make a decision at the right time. Fear will stop you. This will then lead you into emotional instability due to the confusion that indecision gives birth to. It is right to make risk assessments and carry out due diligence before making decisions, but don't let fear dictates your actions.

22. Lack of healing from a past hurt

The Holy Spirit is a healer, but if you reject His healing, (for example, by holding onto bitterness and unforgiveness) you will be keeping past hurts fresh in your memory. When people have not received healing from the hurts they carry, the past begins to control their present. They live under the fear of re-occurrences of past hurts. This is the bondage of fear.

> *Brethren, I count not myself to have apprehended: but this one thing I do, forgetting those things which are behind, and reaching forth unto those things which are before, I press toward the mark...*
> PHILIPPIANS 3:13-14

For you to be able to move forward in your life, you need to be healed of past hurts. Those who are still nursing the hurts of the past are still under fear and trembling of similar situations taking place today. You might have been hurt through a mistake you made, but that does not mean that you will always make the same mistake. Therefore, stop expecting and imagining a re-occurrence of the past hurt in your life.

23. Staying in a wrong relationship

There are people who stay in a relationship despite being fully aware that it is damaging for them. They feel that a bad relationship is better than no relationship at all. They fear loneliness and being unloved more than the abuse or hurts they are experiencing. But if you stay in a wrong relationship that is repeatedly hurting you, you will always live under the fear of being hurt. Such a relationship will become a breeding ground for fear, wrong thoughts and emotional instability. Fear will gain constant control of your behaviour in such a relationship.

In 1 Samuel 16, David came into the service of King Saul. He served Saul for many years, during which David's life was repeatedly threatened by Saul, but there came a point where he fled from serving Saul and never came back. In all the time David stayed under the service of Saul, David would no doubt be discharging his responsibilities with extra caution produced by fear. If you stay in a wrong relationship that constantly threatens your physical or emotional wellbeing, you will live in constant fear of physical or emotional harm.

24. Excessive respect for opponents

If you exaggerate the strength of your opposition, the fear of facing such opposition will grip you. It is difficult to take on an enemy you already believe is stronger than you. If you overestimate the strength of your enemy it will open the door for the devil to start attacking your mind with fear of defeat.

> *And there we saw the giants, the sons of Anak, which come of the giants: and we were in our own sight as grasshoppers, and so we were in their sight.* NUMBERS 13:33

In this story; the Israelites exaggerated the size of their enemy and that diminished them in their own sight. In reality, it is fear that diminished them in their own sight. When you only see strength in your enemy, fear will make you see only weakness in yourself. If you don't want fear to grip you, stop magnifying the strength of your enemy.

25. Believing the captives

Those who have been captured by fear will make you like them if you believe their story. For example, if you accept that those who have failed in a certain endeavour are just like you, then, you will see yourself failing in the same endeavour. The spirit of fear is transmissible from one person to another.

> *And the officers shall speak further unto the people, and they shall say, What man is there that is fearful and fainthearted? Let him go and return unto his house, lest his brethren's heart faint as well as his heart.* DEUTERONOMY 20:8

In this verse, the officers told the men to go home if they were afraid, because their fear would rub off on the rest of the army if they stayed. It indicates that those already captured by the spirit of fear have the capacity to make other people afraid. Therefore, avoid listening to the stories of those under fear because they could transmit the same spirit into your mind.

26. Low self-esteem

To have low self-esteem is to feel unworthy, unqualified and incompetent. Such a person lacks self-confidence. With low self-esteem there is a lack of courage, born out of fear.

> *And there we saw the giants, the sons of Anak, which come of the giants: and we were in our own sight as grasshoppers, and so we were in their sight.* NUMBERS 13:33

In this verse the Israelites described themselves as grasshoppers when comparing themselves with their enemies. Such low self-esteem became the breeding ground for fear, wrong perception and a defeatist attitude. This stole their courage to face their enemies. The more you develop low self-esteem the more you will be afraid to face challenges in life. If you describe yourself badly, the devil will describe you worse. This creates fear in you as you begin to imagine and expect all kinds of defeats and disasters that will probably never happen.

Chapter 4

FEAR IS A STOPPER

A stopper is a device that can be used to close and open something, or put an end to something. Fear is a stopper. It can close an opening to block the manifestation of what is inside, or it can terminate a race that somebody is about to win.

Examples of where fear is a stopper include the following:

1. Potential

If you give in to fear, it will prevent you from manifesting the potential God has placed in you. You must not allow fear to intimidate you and stop you from engaging in any exercise that could enable you to develop new skills, explore your gifts or utilise a talent that has lain dormant. Due to fear, many people have never engaged in the activities that would have helped them to discover their hidden potential.

Whenever fear prevents you from attempting something, be aware that the devil is attacking your mind so as to hinder you from discovering the gifts of God inside you. You can't discover yourself unless you get involved in certain activities, such as those that stretch you and take you out of your comfort zone. But the devil is always afraid of your manifestation as a son or daughter of God because such a manifestation is a product of self-discovery. Fear is a stopper that prevents you from discovering your God-given potential.

2. Vision

Due to the fear that they wouldn't have the resources needed to fulfil a vision, many people have missed their calling. The devil threatened them from the outset that they would never be able to obtain all the resources necessary to advance their vision.

Whenever you want to try a new thing and the first worry that comes to your mind is your lack of resources, be aware that the devil is trying to scare you out of completing your vision. Don't let the devil do that. Even in your lack of resources, press forward with faith and very soon, things will begin to fall into place. God will not give you a mission without supplying the resources. You may have nothing to start with, but if God is in it, you have all that you need. Don't wait for all the resources before you start. *"My God shall supply all your need according to his riches in glory by Christ Jesus"* (Philippians 4:9).

3. Exploration

Exploration is about discovering new things. Fear will not let you explore new things because it will threaten you with a series of uncertainties. There are many untapped opportunities around you, but to discover them will require taking risks and the devil will attack your mind with doubts that you do not have what it takes or the fear that the dangers are too great. If you yield to such threats, you will not be able to break new ground and discover treasures in hidden places.

4. Status quo

This means the current state of things. Fear can force you to keep to the status quo. It will not let you try new ideas or methods. Fear always likes to make its victims the lovers of the old and haters of the new. That's because when you try a new idea or method, you may discover a better way of doing the same thing. Whenever you try to resist change, it could be because of the fear of change rather than because the change is wrong.

5. Good health

Fear can stop you from enjoying good health. If you allow fear to keep on dictating your life, it will start causing your body systems to malfunction. For example, it has been discovered that fear can cause a series of aches in the human body, high blood pressure, chronic fatigue, exhaustion, low energy heartburn, indigestion, breathing problems, chest pain, angina and other medical conditions. You will need to stop your fear now before it stops your good health.

6. Relationships

Fear can stop you from engaging in good relationships. If you begin a new relationship with the fear that your bitter experience from past relationships may re-occur, then, you will hinder yourself from enjoying every blessing planted in the new relationship. Fear will make you become irrational, both in thinking and action. This will prevent the free flowing of blessings God might want to bring to the new relationship. God has destined many relationships to be a blessing to people, but they have turned sour because of the carrying over of bad experiences and a negative mind-set. Don't let fears stop a new relationship if it is a good and godly one. Arise and stop the fear now.

7. Divine peace

God has given us His peace but fear can rob you of enjoying it. You can't experience peace when you see danger in everything due to fear. The peace of God is beyond human understanding because it rules above everything that can threaten the existence of man. The peace of God is heavenly. Therefore, with the peace of God, there should be no fear. But you will still need to make a decision whether to enjoy this divine peace to its fullest or not.

If you refuse to make a conscious effort to defeat your fear, you will not be able to enjoy the full blessings of divine peace from heaven. God's peace is given to enable you to say no to every kind of fear the enemy may want to bring into your mind. Do not let fear stop the operation of the peace of God in your life. Arise against your fear.

8. Possessing your possession

This is to take hold of what God has freely given to you. But in many situations you will need to fight in order to claim what is yours or keep what is yours. This kind of fighting is not only needed at the beginning but all through the process of possessing your possession. Fear can stop you from fighting. Some people start out well, but as the battle rages on, they surrender to fear and the enemy steals their possession.

For example, a promotion at work may be yours but sometimes you may need to fight in prayer or faith in order to receive it. The enemy can use the weapon of fear to stop you from going through the process that is required to obtain your promotion. Not all promotions are of God, but don't lose out on one that is from Him because of fear. Commit the application process and interview, if involved in the process, into the hands of God and believe that God will be on your side and give you success if He wants you to have the promotion.

9. Fulfilling your days

God's plan for you is that you are able to fulfil your days by living to old age in good health and prosperity. Unfortunately, if you allow fear to rule you, it will put your entire life into such a torment that your life will be shortened by anxiety. Fear can even make you so afraid of old age that you want to die young. Fear can also hinder you from taking the good steps to help make your life better and gracious. Fear can set into motion; a variety of toxic processes both within and outside your body, capable of shortening your lifespan. If you desire to live long and see your children's children, you will need to get rid of fear so that your body systems can function peacefully and keep you in sound body and mind.

10. Winning the battle you're supposed to win

Fear can make you lose many battles that you have the ability to win. It makes you quit and lets the opponent rob you of your victory. It is one thing to start a journey with boldness and faith, it is another thing to persevere on the journey with the same boldness and faith until it is completed. Some people start the race very well but when challenges increase, fear grips them and they turn back.

If you don't want the enemy to rob you of potential victories, you will need to ensure that you don't give in to fear at any stage of the process.

11. Keeping the door of opportunities open

It is possible to locate a door of opportunity and still not be able to access the opportunities inside it. Many people have come to their door of opportunity but fear prevents them from opening it. Some people are afraid to push their way forward in life due to fear. In some situations, you will need to apply force to make certain doors open, but if you are too afraid, to do that, the door will remain shut against you.

For example, if you are attending an interview for employment but you allow the faces and appearances of the interviewers to intimidate you, you will lack boldness to present your good opinions and promote yourself. Fear may make you lose that job. Do not let fear keep robbing you of blessings that are supposed to be yours; arise against your fear.

12. Avoiding procrastination

Procrastination is the habit of delaying an action. Fear can make you delay an important step, and then; you may lose out on something that would have yielded blessings for you. That is why it is important to identify why you are delaying to take action. Could it be due to laziness or is it fear? If you are procrastinating due to the fear of possible negative outcomes, then you will need to fight your fear.

13. Making a difference

In some situations, God orchestrates your stay in a certain place with the aim of using you as an agent of change. If you allow Him, He will make positive differences in the place where you are, though you. But if you are too afraid to follow His leading, fear may stop you from fulfilling your purpose in that place. For example, due to the fear of opposition from other people, you may not be courageous enough to make a stand about certain wrong things in your work place, and so positive differences won't be made. To be an agent of change will require being bold enough to get involved in certain things in the area where God has placed you. Do not let fear side-line you.

14. Avoiding ministerial failure

Fear can make us fail in the work God has called us to do for Him. If we allow fear to dictate our actions, we will find that we cannot do all the work we need to do. In fact, we may never get started in the ministry in the first place. There are many ways in which fear prevents a ministry beginning or makes it less effective. Whether it's a fear of lack of resources, or fear of the resources not being available at the right time, or fear of what others will say or do, the work we are called-to will never get off the ground if we don't resist fear.

The devil is not only an agent of fear but also a deceiver. The same devil who frightens you into believing that you can't start the work now because you don't have enough resources, is the same one who will also lie to you to wait for the perfect time. He knows that perfect time will never come. If you keep listening to his fear and deception, you may never fulfil your ministry. Whatever God has called you to do for Him, start in faith – because He who has called you; is faithful.

15. Avoiding demobilisation

To be demobilised is a military term for being taken out of active service. But it simply means to bring to a standstill. Fear can demobilise a person. It can make somebody redundant.

When fear is allowed in, even a journey that has been progressing well can suddenly come to a standstill. Fear is a stopper. It can halt any process or journey. When you suddenly abandon a good idea, it may be due to fear. When you suddenly feel like closing down a project that was previously moving on well, you may be under the influence of fear. When you suddenly lose interest in forging ahead in a certain project, it may be fear threatening you. If it is fear, you will need to deal with it and not give in to its power.

16. Avoiding conditioning

Conditioning is a situation where the way you react under certain situations becomes predictable. This may include your manner of thinking or action. Fear can condition you so that in certain environments; you only reason or act in the same way, every time. This makes you exhibit a pattern both in thought and action.

Fear can stop you from being dynamic and flexible under certain situations. For example, a person who is afraid of travelling by aeroplane will exhibit a predictable pattern of thinking and action whenever he is asked to travel by aeroplane. Even if there is no reason to suspect a plane is in danger and every safety regulation is in place, the person will still not be able to think or act differently. Fear has conditioned him. Such a person can be described as having a phobia, because there is virtually no reason to be afraid in such a situation. Statistically, it's still safer to travel by air than by car.

Therefore, if you find it hard to change your thoughts and actions in response to certain things, irrespective of the good reasons for supporting the change, it may be that fear has programmed you to function in such a manner. You will need to deal with your fear.

17. Commitment

This is a state or quality of being dedicated to a cause or activity. Such a cause could be a business or academic project, or an investment or training for life improvement – anything you are determined to achieve. Fear can stop you from being committed. Some people show commitment to a cause as long as the situation is favourable, but as soon as it becomes challenging, their commitment start to dwindle. This could be due to unexpected hurdles that suddenly appear. Fear of crossing such hurdles may dampen their spirit and they lose interest and commitment. Therefore, when you suddenly start losing interest in whatever has been making you active and committed, it may be due to fear. Fear is a stopper; don't let it stop your commitment to a good cause. If you can keep your commitment, remain active and strong in the face of hurdles, you will suddenly discover the means of overcoming them.

18. Speaking out

Fear can stop you from speaking out due to oppression. There are many people today who are suffering in silence because they are too afraid to speak against whatever or whoever is oppressing them. Sometimes, the forces of oppression have instilled so much fear into the minds of their victims that it will take a very courageous victim to speak out. Fear makes you justify your silence and rationalise why you can't find freedom, despite your discomfort. Do not allow your life to be made miserable by oppressive people. You will need to face your fear and speak up for help. No matter how powerful your oppressors are, they are defeatable. When you speak out, you give others in the same situation the courage to do the same, and you may even shame your oppressors into changing their behaviour. But whether change comes easily or not, there will be no change at all if you remain silent.

19. Being loving

Fear can stop you from loving a person. When your mind is filled with a series of negative possibilities about a relationship, you may gradually start losing love for the person you love. When you begin to give more attention to the possibility of disappointment in a relationship, you may stop showing love to the person. When you become unnecessarily suspicious of your partner, you may stop loving him or her. When you suddenly start imagining yourself becoming a loser in a relationship or believing it will fall apart, it could be that the enemy is planting fear in your heart regarding that relationship.

If you allow the negative possibilities of your relationship to make you afraid, you will water down the spirit of love operating in the relationship. Therefore, when you notice that you are losing affection for a person you are in love with, it may be due to fear. It could be that you are listening to the devil who is attacking your mind with a series of negative possible outcomes in the relationship. Fear is a stopper; you will need to resist it, otherwise, it will stop your good relationship from continuing.

20. Right decisions

Sometimes, after making the right decision about something, we allow fear to creep in, and we may feel like reversing the decision we have just made. So, if this happens to you, you will need to thoroughly investigate your reason for a change of mind about your decision, to check whether you are right to change it or if it is just fear driving your emotions.

For example, if you have made a decision to bless somebody financially, the enemy can start attacking your mind with the fear of being able to afford such a gift. 'What if your situation changes and you need the money yourself?' he asks. If you listen to this voice of fear, you may eventually change your mind and stop being a blessing to the person you have promised to help.

Whenever you make a decision, ensure that there is conviction in your heart for such a decision, and also make another decision never to alter it purely on the basis of fear. This will help you to resist the fear the enemy may bring to deceive you into changing your decision. Do not let the winds of fear keep swaying you around from one decision to another.

21. Being yourself

Fear can lead people to be 'unreal' – to pretend to be the person you are not. Some people try to be more like someone else they admire or think is popular, because they are afraid that they are not good enough to be liked or loved. People are afraid of not being accepted by others due to various faults they see in themselves or think they see in themselves, and so, they feel they can't be themselves when around others.

It is the enemy who makes people afraid of being real. Those who allow such fears in their hearts will start making up new personalities to please those from whom they are seeking acceptance. The major problem in this camouflaging is that you will always struggle to keep your 'faked personality' because it is all an act that is hard to keep up. Very soon the same people you are trying to please will notice irregularities in your performance and conclude that you are an unstable or unreliable personality. Do not let fear tear you apart. Be yourself. Your real friends will accept you for who you are, and those who are not really on your side will never accept you – irrespective of how good a 'show' you can put on.

22. Liberty

Fear can remove your liberty if you allow it. Fear attacks its victims by making them practise 'self-imprisonment'. In your self-created prison, you will always miss out on certain things in life. For example, due to fear, some people lock themselves behind closed doors during certain periods of the day, in order to escape their imaginary danger. Others avoid passing along certain roads due to an imaginary danger or a past incident. Due to fear, you may choose not to take a job with a particular organisation due to some evil you imagine is in the work-place.

The more you allow fear to dictate your life, the more you will lose your freedom. God has given you His Spirit of love, not a spirit of fear (2 Timothy 1:7), and His perfect love casts out all fear (1 John 4:18), so ask the Holy Spirit to take control of your life and cast out your fears.

If you critically consider some fears, you will realise that you made them up in your mind—they are unfounded.

23. Self-trust

You were created wonderfully and beautifully by God. As a child of God, you are loaded with a lot of potential and giftings. You are actually stronger than you or anybody could think. The Bible describes you as part of a holy nation, made in image of God, more than a conqueror, etc. All these descriptions are true and they should create in you; a sense of self-worth, then, you can live your life with self-confidence.

Unfortunately, the enemy will attempt to make you feel worthless and weak. If you accept this lie from the enemy, you will lose confidence to face the issues of life, because you feel inadequate. No matter how strong your desire to win in life, if you lose self-confidence, then, fear will make you run away from the battlefield.

Some people have great self-confidence at the beginning of an endeavour, but when the devil starts convincing them that they don't have what it takes to succeed, fear grips their minds and they quit. Never allow fear to steal your confidence because once it is stolen, it will take a lot of effort to regain.

24. Sensitivity to the Spirit

When we have the ability to react or behave in certain situations without having to think about it, we call it instinctive behaviour. It can be useful, but can also be misguided. As a Christian, you have the Spirit of the Lord living inside of you – and it is the Holy Spirit we should try to 'tune into', so that we instinctively follow His ways. In fact, the Holy Spirit's job is to make us more like Christ, so that it is natural for us to behave like Jesus rather than follow our fallen human nature.

Unfortunately, if you start doubting the Lord's presence with you and work within you, you will allow fear to hinder you from acting wisely in many situations. Fear makes you unavailable for the touch of the Spirit of God. A person caged by fear will be naturally insensitive to the voice of the Spirit of God that dwells inside us. Such a person will be hard to move into an action that he or she has not prepared for. Fear destroys spiritual sensitivity. When God calls, you may not hear, because you are absorbed with your fears.

25. Excitement

It is possible to start a journey with excitement and motivation. But if fear is allowed to creep into the mind, the excitement and motivation may disappear. Fear can kill the fire of excitement that the Holy Spirit ignites inside you.

When you stop listening to the inner voice of the Spirit of God and start reasoning with the devil about a possible danger, then your spirit will lose excitement and motivation. Therefore, when you suddenly start feeling cold towards things that used to excite and motivate you, it may be that you have allowed the enemy to make you afraid.

For example, many people enter into marriage with excitement and hope, but after a few years on the journey, the enemy starts bombarding them with fears of problems coming into their marriage, and they become very cold towards their partner. This could be the beginning of a marital crisis. Do not let fears stop your excitement. Fight your fear to remain positive. Refuse to fall into the trap of a fear-filled imagination and false expectations.

26. Thinking well of others

Fear can make you start thinking of other people as a threat or as insincere. You may think this way because the devil has highlighted some of their words or behaviour that you feel is wrong. No one is perfect, so there is always something the devil can use to tempt you into feeling afraid of them.

This fear can make you start seeing more and more evil in these people, and you begin to distrust them even when they are being honest with you. Whenever the devil wants to destroy a relationship, he will start attacking the weakest link in the relationship, and he arouses your suspicions and calls your attention to things that do not exist but are made up by him. Too much close examination with a negative mind-set will definitely make you start seeing bad things that do not exist in these people.

If you notice that you are feeling very negative towards people around you, it may be for a good reason or it could be due to the devil working on your mind. If you give in to the fear of possible dangers from people, you will spend most of your daylight hours thinking about them and analysing their actions and words towards you. It is better to choose to think good about people and stop looking for the bad about them, unless they do behave in obviously evil ways. Even then, recognise that there is good and bad in everyone.

27. Seeing the big picture

To see the big picture in a situation is to see the most important parts of it and its connectivity to other vital parts. Fear can make you keep focusing on irrelevant or minor parts of a situation. The part of the situation that frightens you most will definitely consume most of your attention, while you ignore what is most important in the situation. Such fear may hinder you from seeing the great blessings that will come from the completion of a particular project or course of action, and so prevent you from embarking on it. Seeing the big picture may help you see that the risk is worth taking.

If the big picture reveals the great blessings that may come from taking a particular course of action, then, you will be more willing to fight the fear that would stop you. But if fear of the small part of the picture has consumed you, you will not be able to see or appreciate the great reward that could come from moving ahead. Do not let your fear blindfold you.

28. Being the person God created you to be

Fear can stop you from developing into the person God created you to be. The more you give in to fear, the more you will lock up the potential inside of you. You will need courage to fight the battle of life and it is this battle that will bring your hidden potential to the surface. The more you allow fear to make you run from the challenges of life, the more you will be unable to discover your real self.

The devil loves to attack us with fear so that we won't grow into our gifting and acquire God-given abilities. Fear will stop you from stepping out; into new things, so that you will not discover who you really are in the Lord. Fear can prevent you from discovering your uniqueness. Unfortunately, until you discover your uniqueness, you are vulnerable to the mistake of trying to be like someone else, which is a path to failure. Fear is a stopper and it is able to stop a person from being great in life.

29. Seeing a better option

If your fear takes complete control, you will not be able to see the better options opening to you in a situation. In many circumstances of life, there are several options open to you, but too much attention to your fear will blind you from seeing the better choices. Fear paralyses the creative power inside a person.

If your fear has gained control of you, when you face challenges, your creative ability may be locked up within you, and you won't be able to figure out any better options. When one method doesn't work, it is likely that another method will work, but fear can make you conclude that there is no other way of achieving a cause. You will probably be afraid of investing further resources into the cause.

So if you notice that you have lost creativity in a cause, check if the spirit of fear is at work on you.

30. Trusting God

Fear can stop you trusting God. If your faith starts wavering, it could be due to fear. If you stop believing that with God; all things are possible, it could be due to fear. So if you notice that your faith in God's faithfulness or reliability is failing, you may need to deal with the spirit of fear.

Chapter 5

HOW TO STOP YOUR FEAR

───────■───────

Fear is stoppable. It can be defeated. You can stop being afraid. You can stop your fear from controlling your thinking, imagination, meditation, expectations, actions, confessions and decisions.

In this chapter we will use the encounter of David against Goliath as a case study to enable us understand how to defeat our fear.

> *And there went out a champion out of the camp of the Philistines, named Goliath, of Gath, whose height was six cubits and a span. And he had an helmet of brass upon his head, and he was armed with a coat of mail; and the weight of the coat was five thousand shekels of brass. And he had greaves of brass upon his legs, and a target of brass between his shoulders. And the staff of his spear was like a weaver's beam; and his spear's head weighed six hundred shekels of iron: and one bearing a shield went before him. And he stood and cried unto the armies of Israel, and said unto them, Why are ye come out to set your battle in array? Am not I a Philistine, and ye servants to Saul? Choose you a man for you, and let him come down to me. If he be able to fight with me, and to kill me, then will we be your servants: but if I prevail against him, and kill him, then shall ye be our servants, and serve us. And the Philistine said, I defy the armies of Israel this day; give me a man, that we may fight together. When Saul and all Israel heard those words of the Philistine, they were dismayed, and greatly afraid.* 1 SAMUEL 17:4-11

In the story of David and Goliath, the Philistines came against the nation of Israel with their hero Goliath boasting and threatening the whole nation.

> *And the Philistine drew near morning and evening, and presented himself forty days.* 1 SAMUEL 17:16

This verse states that Goliath kept challenging Israel for 40 days. So, for 40 days the whole army of Israel was hearing the threats and taunts of Goliath. This is the strategy that hell used to control and dominate the thoughts, expectations and imagination of the whole nation of Israel. As Israel kept on hearing and seeing the same thing for 40 days, in their eyes Goliath would have appeared bigger and stronger every day. The fear built up as Goliath no doubt grew in confidence and made more threats, as no Israelite dared to accept his challenge.

Whatever fear holds, your attention will appear bigger than it really is. It is therefore not surprising that even King Saul exaggerated the strength of Goliath; he saw him as undefeatable. The whole nation of Israel went silent for many days. Nobody had the confidence to stand against their enemy. They were greatly afraid of Goliath. The fear you delay dealing with will always appear bigger and stronger as time goes on. Such fear will dominate your life in a negative way.

It is practically impossible for you to ignore thoughts that keep on coming to your mind for many days. If you have no solution to it, you are likely to accept it as your cross to carry.

Goliath in this story is the embodiment of many fears. Let us examine some of these fears that Goliath represented.

1. Fear of man

Goliath was a man, not a spirit. Those who feared him feared man.

> *The LORD is on my side; I will not fear: what can man do unto me?* PSALM 118:6

This verse encourages us to stop fearing other people, irrespective of their strength. After all, God is always on our side, so who can stand against Him? One with God is always a majority.

2. Fear of defeat

Goliath represents the fear of defeat. Nobody in Israel was courageous enough to stand against Goliath because of the fear of being beaten. That would mean death for the man and slavery for the nation. None of the Israelites could bear the thought of being defeated by the Philistines.

> *Nay, in all these things we are more than conquerors through him that loved us.* ROMANS 8:37

This verse states that you are stronger than your enemy. If Goliath represents a conqueror, you are stronger than him. With God on your side, you can't be defeated by any human enemy. If this Bible verse had been around at Saul's time and he'd read it, maybe he would have accepted Goliath's challenge instead of surrendering to his fears.

3. Fear of death

The Israelites, of course, thought Goliath would kill them if they fought him. David was well aware that he could be killed too, but in faith, he believed that God would enable him to defeat the giant.

> *If he be able to fight with me, and to kill me, then will we be your servants: but if I prevail against him, and kill him, then shall ye be our servants, and serve us.* 1 SAMUEL 17:9

Goliath had come with a threat of death. Nobody was able to rise against him because they were afraid to die.

> *And deliver them who through fear of death were all their lifetime subject to bondage.* HEBREWS 2:15

As a Christian, you have been delivered from the power of death. Until your God-given time to live on earth expires, nothing can kill you. Do not let the enemy use death to make you afraid.

4. Fear of uncertainty

Goliath represented the fear of uncertainty to Israel. Nobody in Israel could predict how the dust would settle regarding the threat of Goliath. Until David killed Goliath, the whole nation was under a cloud of darkness.

> *God is our refuge and strength, a very present help in trouble.* PSALM 46:1

This verse assures us that help is always available whenever we face any trouble. Therefore, our future is certain in God. Whenever you face uncertainty, tell yourself that your God is in charge.

5. Fear of history repeating itself

In the past, before the time of Goliath, the Philistine nation had defeated Israel. So to Israel, Goliath represented the possibility of a past defeat re-occurring. Perhaps many of God's people were asking themselves: "Are the Philistines going to rule over us again?"

Are you facing the fear of a terrible event from your past re-occurring in your life?

> *What do ye imagine against the LORD? He will make an utter end: affliction shall not rise up the second time.* NAHUM 1:9

This verse gives you assurance that evil will not re-occur in your life. If you are worried that something bad from your past is raising its ugly head again, instead of living under fear, stand on this word of promise from God. You can stop this fear.

6. Fear of battle

Goliath represents the fear of battle. The whole nation of Israel was afraid of going into battle against Goliath. They believed that none of them had what it takes to defeat Goliath. They believed that Goliath was stronger than them and a very experienced fighter. Even King Saul told David that Goliath had a lot of experience when it comes to battle.

Is a battle making you afraid? You can stop that fear now.

> *And he said, Hearken ye, all Judah, and ye inhabitants of Jerusalem, and thou king Jehoshaphat, Thus saith the LORD unto you, Be not afraid nor dismayed by reason of this great multitude; for the battle is not yours, but God's.* 2 CHRONICLES 20:15

Any battle that comes against a child of God has directly come against God. You are not expected to fight your own battle by yourself, but you do need to release it into God's hands. Stop the fear of battle now. As Psalm 27:1 says: *"The Lord is the strength of my life; of whom shall I be afraid?"*

7. Fear of gods

Goliath represents the fear of gods. He was fighting in the name of his gods. These gods were demonic powers who the Philistines worshipped, whether they knew they were demons or not.

> *And the Philistine said unto David, Am I a dog, that thou comest to me with staves? And the Philistine cursed David by his gods.*
> 1 SAMUEL 17:43

Goliath cursed David in the name of his gods. Are you afraid of curses? Are you afraid of those who have demonic power? Are you afraid of witches, warlocks, mediums, diviners and anyone who is being used by the devil?

> *Surely there is no enchantment against Jacob, neither is there any divination against Israel: according to this time it shall be said of Jacob and of Israel, What hath God wrought!* NUMBERS 23:23

The Word of God here gives you assurance that no demonic power or consultation will work against you. Therefore, you can stop being afraid of the devil's power. James 4:7 says: *"Resist the devil, and he will flee from you."*

8. Fear of insecurity

Goliath represented the fear of insecurity to the nation of Israel. His existence threatened the security of Israel. Unless Goliath was defeated, Israel would not have any peace or security. Who and what is threatening your security?

> *The eternal God is thy refuge, and underneath are the everlasting arms: and he shall thrust out the enemy from before thee; and shall say, Destroy them.* DEUTERONOMY 33:27

God is your security. And if God is your security, there is no danger that can threaten your existence. You can stop that fear now by standing upon the infallible Word of God.

9. Fear of enslavement

Goliath symbolises the fear of enslavement.

> *If he be able to fight with me, and to kill me, then will we be your servants: but if I prevail against him, and kill him, then shall ye be our servants, and serve us.* 1 SAMUEL 17:9

Goliath made it clear that he had come to take the nation of Israel into slavery. The citizens of Israel would have been very afraid of losing their freedom.

Are you facing the fear of being enslaved?

> *And the LORD shall make thee the head, and not the tail; and thou shalt be above only, and thou shalt not be beneath; if that thou hearken unto the commandments of the LORD thy God, which I command thee this day, to observe and to do them.*
> DEUTERONOMY 28:13

How can you be enslaved when God has already declared you the head? You can stop that fear now by claiming your covenant right to always be the head, not the tail. You will always be on top and never at the bottom.

10. Fear of danger

Goliath represents the fear of danger. He was brutal and ruthless. He had come to do as much harm as possible to the people of Israel.

> *Yea, though I walk through the valley of the shadow of death, I will fear no evil: for thou art with me; thy rod and thy staff they comfort me.* PSALM 23:4

God's presence shields His children from every kind of danger. When you walk in the assurance of God's presence surrounding you, you will fear no evil.

11. Fear of intimidation

Goliath was intimidating the Israelite army. Everything about Goliath was intimidating – his height, dress, and armour:

> *And there went out a champion out of the camp of the Philistines, named Goliath, of Gath, whose height was six cubits and a span. And he had an helmet of brass upon his head, and he was armed with a coat of mail; and the weight of the coat was five thousand shekels of brass. And he had greaves of brass upon his legs, and a target of brass between his shoulders. And the staff of his spear was like a weaver's beam; and his spear's head weighed six hundred shekels of iron: and one bearing a shield went before him.* 1 SAMUEL 17:4-7

His appearance in the battle made the nation of Israel weak at the knees. Are you afraid of any sort of intimidation? Is anything making you feel inadequate?

> *Not that we are sufficient of ourselves to think any thing as of ourselves; but our sufficiency is of God...* 2 CORINTHIANS 3:5

What makes you sufficient for victory is not your personal skills or qualifications but your trust in Christ Jesus. Therefore, you will need to stop the fear that is making you feeling inadequate to face your opponent.

12. Fear of disinheritance

To Israel, Goliath represented the fear of losing their inheritance. The Promised Land God gave to Israel as their inheritance was threatened by Goliath. If Goliath had defeated Israel, the Philistines would have taken over the land of Israel and governed the whole nation.

Are you facing the fear of losing what God has given you?

> *For I will defend this city to save it for mine own sake, and for my servant David's sake.* ISAIAH 37:35

This verse assures us that whatever God gives us, He is able to protect for us. You can stop the fear of losing what God has given you by standing upon this Bible verse. Use it for your encouragement.

13. Fear of words

Goliath represents the fear of words. He spoke threatening words to Israel. His speech was intended to create fear, and it was succeeding. In his words, Goliath showed disrespect for the God of Israel and boasted that he would defeat Israel's champion and enslave the nation. When he spoke, everybody went silent.

> *Who is he that saith, and it cometh to pass, when the Lord commandeth it not?* LAMENTATIONS 3:37

Despite all men's boasting, none of their words will be fulfilled unless God allows it. You can stop the fear of words that somebody spoke into your mind, knowing full well that the fulfilment of such words solely depends on God.

14. Fear of change

Goliath represents the fear of change. If Goliath had defeated Israel, there would have been huge change in the lives of the people of Israel – change for the worse. No doubt, the people were imagining all the terrible changes the Philistines would make in Israel if Goliath won.

Are you afraid of change? The reality of life is that the only thing that never changes is change itself. There will always be changes happening in your life.

> *For I am the LORD, I change not; therefore ye sons of Jacob are not consumed.* MALACHI 3:6

Whatever change may unfold in your life, what matters is that your God never changes. Because God always remains the same, He is able to protect you in the ever changing world in which we live, and His love is constant. Don't fear change: your God never changes.

15. Fear of the future

With the arrival of Goliath in Israel, the future became unpredictable to Israel. All the people had dreams and visions they were chasing before Goliath came on the scene, but all those futures were now under threat. If Goliath won, their nation faced a bleak future. There was no longer any guarantee that the people's hopes would be fulfilled: in fact, there might have been no future at all for them.

Are you facing a situation that is threatening the future of your marriage, career, vision, dreams, ministry, etc.?

> *For I know the thoughts that I think toward you, saith the LORD, thoughts of peace, and not of evil, to give you an expected end.*
> JEREMIAH 29:11

The Word of God is assuring you that you will reach the goals God wants for you. Your future is guaranteed in God. Irrespective of any fear, God's plans for your life will be fulfilled.

16. Fear of the crowd

Goliath represents the fear of the crowd. Goliath did not come alone to attack the nation of Israel. He came with a large army of fellow Philistines, to offer him support if necessary. This implies that apart from Goliath, there is the possibility of many other enemies to fight in the battle. Whoever rises against Goliath directly will also rise against the Philistines who came with him.

Are you afraid of those people who support your enemies?

> *And he answered, Fear not: for they that be with us are more than they that be with them.* 2 KINGS 6:16

The Word of God above assures us that we have more supporters than our enemies. No matter how large the number of those on your enemy's side, you have more supporters on your side. You can stop that fear right now.

17. Fear of abuse

Goliath represents the fear of abuse. Many Israelite people who heard his threats would have been imagining the scale of possible abuse they would suffer if the Philistines captured Israel and ruled over them. Are you also suffering from the fear of abuse in your life?

> *For the oppression of the poor, for the sighing of the needy, now will I arise, saith the LORD; I will set him in safety from him that puffeth at him.* PSALM 12:5

God will always rise against any sort of abuse. Do not be afraid of abuse for your God is on your side. If someone is threatening you with abuse, seek help from other Christians or/and go to the police if it is a threat of physical or sexual abuse. Do not live in fear but take action to end the threat of abuse.

18. Fear of negative possibilities

Goliath represents the fear of many negative possibilities for Israel. The list of possible disastrous outcomes for Israel was very large. There was no limit to what the devil brought into the minds of those who witnessed the threats of Goliath.

And if we dwell on all the negative possibilities for life, then, we are wasting time and energy that could be spent pursuing positive possibilities, as well as living in fear of things that might never happen. Remember that with all these things…

… they are not real.

Notice that all the fears we have just looked at are not real. Each is a forecast, a product of prediction and imagination. Fear is about the possibility of what may happen, not what has actually happened. It is therefore important for you to know that what is making you afraid is in your mind. This is the reason why if you want to be free from any sort of fear, you will need to deal with yourself internally.

David stopped the fear of Goliath:

> *And David put his hand in his bag, and took thence a stone, and slang it, and smote the Philistine in his forehead, that the stone sunk into his forehead; and he fell upon his face to the earth. So David prevailed over the Philistine with a sling and with a stone, and smote the Philistine, and slew him; but there was no sword in the hand of David. Therefore David ran, and stood upon the Philistine, and took his sword, and drew it out of the sheath thereof, and slew him, and cut off his head therewith. And when the Philistines saw their champion was dead, they fled.*
> 1 SAMUEL 17:49-51

In the Bible story, David stopped the fear of Goliath. He killed Goliath with his own sword. The threat against the nation of Israel that had lasted 40 days finally came to an end.

If David could do it, you can do it too. You can stop your fear. If David could destroy the fear that brought the whole nation to a standstill, you also can stop your fear before it stops you.

HOW TO STOP YOUR FEAR

Let us examine how David stopped the fear of Goliath that came against the whole nation of Israel.

1. Know your enemy

> *For God hath not given us the spirit of fear; but of power, and of love, and of a sound mind.* 2 TIMOTHY 1:7

If God has not given us the spirit of fear, the question is: where does fear come from?

> *Forasmuch then as the children are partakers of flesh and blood, he also himself likewise took part of the same; that through death he might destroy him that had the power of death, that is, the devil; and deliver them who through fear of death were all their lifetime subject to bondage.* HEBREWS 2:14-15

Everything that makes you afraid can be traced back to the devil. It is the devil who attacks your mind with fear.

> *Ye are of your father the devil, and the lusts of your father ye will do. He was a murderer from the beginning, and abode not in the truth, because there is no truth in him. When he speaketh a lie, he speaketh of his own: for he is a liar, and the father of it.* JOHN 8:44

If fear is from the devil; and we know that the devil is a liar, then, it implies that fear is not real. Therefore, you must know that every evil possibility making you afraid is not real. They are all fabricated from hell to steal your peace. In some situations, the devil gathers up some fake evidence in order to convince you to accept the reality of the fear he is bringing into your mind. Such evidence could come from past experiences that have hurt you. He will magnify all this evidence and keep on attacking your mind to accept his lies.

Therefore, what is actually making you afraid is the devil, not the situation that you fear. It is the devil acting behind the scenes who is making you afraid of that person or that situation, of death or loss. That devil is a liar, perverting and continually twisting the situation in your mind to present it in the way that will frighten you.

> *And David spake to the men that stood by him, saying, What shall be done to the man that killeth this Philistine, and taketh*

> *away the reproach from Israel? For who is this uncircumcised Philistine, that he should defy the armies of the living God?*
> 1 SAMUEL 17:26

In this verse, David identified the real enemy. He described him as an uncircumcised Philistine. As an uncircumcised man, Goliath had no share in the benefit of the covenant God made with Israel. Furthermore, being uncircumcised made Goliath unclean under the Law. Fear is always unclean in its operation – very dirty. Every thought and imagination that fear brings into your mind is unclean, which means it can't be from God. Therefore, what is frightening you is not from God, it is from the devil – the father of all lies. God has already promised His children that whatever is unclean shall be separated from their land.

Now that you know that your fear can't be from God and that it is from the devil, you are on a better ground to stand against it.

David knew who Goliath really was. For you to stop your fear, you will need to identify and understand your fear. You can't stop what you don't know. Are you facing fear of man or of the unknown? Check out what is really making you afraid and all the lies about evil possibilities that may be flooding your mind. They are all unclean and can't be from God. This is your ground for a victory over your fear.

2. Identify your covenant position

When David declared Goliath as uncircumcised, he was directly declaring that he (David) was circumcised – a member of the family of God with covenant benefits. That is, David saw himself as being in a stronger position than Goliath, because of God's covenant with Israel.

> *Awake, awake; put on thy strength, O Zion; put on thy beautiful garments, O Jerusalem, the holy city: for henceforth there shall*

> *no more come into thee the uncircumcised and the unclean.*
> ISAIAH 52:1

In this verse, God promised Israel that; the time would come when He would not allow any unclean people to take over Jerusalem again. In your covenant position, you are in a position of enjoying support from God to get rid of every unclean thing troubling your life, including your fear. This implies that when you rise to stop your fear, God will grant you support because it falls within the context of His word of promise to you as His child. Therefore, you can stop your fear if you chose to do so, for help is available from heaven.

3. Question your fear

> *And David spake to the men that stood by him, saying, What shall be done to the man that killeth this Philistine, and taketh away the reproach from Israel? for who is this uncircumcised Philistine, that he should defy the armies of the living God?*
> 1 SAMUEL 17:26

In this verse, we see David questioning the strength and claim of Goliath against the God of Israel.

For you to stop your fear, you will need to question it. It is when you start probing and analysing your fear that you will discover that it is a tissue of lies and fabrications. Many people live under fear because they never ask themselves questions about what is making them afraid. When you question your fear, you may discover that it is totally unreasonable, or at least; exaggerated. You may also discover that what is making you afraid is actually afraid of you.

For example, many wild animals are more afraid of us than we are of them, despite our overblown fears about them. And that man that you are really afraid of may be trying to frighten you because he is actually afraid of you himself.

Through questioning, you may be able to raise an interesting logical question that will defeat your fear. For example, the fact that you have suffered a loss in the past does not necessarily mean that you will suffer a loss again in the future. Therefore, why should you be afraid of making another attempt at something, simply because of past failure? For one thing, this time, you will have learned from your defeat and so should be better equipped to succeed.

Question your fear.

4. Speak out your truth

Your truth is what God has taught and showed you in the past – your personal encounters with God and revelations from Him. Truth can't be defeated because it is the real thing in any situation, it is what you have actually witnessed and experienced.

> *And Saul said to David, Thou art not able to go against this Philistine to fight with him: for thou art but a youth, and he a man of war from his youth.* 1 SAMUEL 17:33

This statement from Saul was an assumption. It was only based on what Saul knew about David and Goliath – but there was a lot more that he didn't know. Saul was just giving his opinion, not a truth from God, so it couldn't be regarded as the truth, or at least not the whole truth, because the situation may have proved him wrong – and so it turned out. Saul hadn't taken David's faith and courage into account.

> *And I went out after him, and smote him, and delivered it out of his mouth: and when he arose against me, I caught him by his beard, and smote him, and slew him. Thy servant slew both the lion and the bear: and this uncircumcised Philistine shall be as one of them, seeing he hath defied the armies of the living God.*
> 1 SAMUEL 17:35-36

Here, David spoke the truth, because he was relating what had actually happened to him. He was sharing what God had taught and showed him in the past, through his encounters with lions and bears.

To stop your fear, you will need to shift your attention away from the probabilities and focus on the facts. All the evil possibilities the devil brings into your mind are all a game of chance: they do not exist. The truth is what God has taught and showed you in the past – your personal encounters with Him.

For example, when you search into your past you will discover that God has proved Himself so much, to the extent that you can actually be confident that He will arise for you again and again. If God has delivered you from danger in the past, why should you now believe a word of probability from the devil?

Is he making you afraid of an accident so that you will avoid travelling to important events? If the devil is doing this, you can easily reply to him that your God will travel with you and there is no way God will be with you and watch you get involved in an accident. Because God has done it before in your life, this is the truth, not just a probability.

Your personal experience was arranged by God to put you in a position where you will be able to debunk every lie and threat from the devil. That experience is vital. When the devil brings fearful thoughts into your mind, neutralise them all with the truth. Fear is about probability but your personal experience with God is the reality, the truth.

5. Fight spiritual problems with spiritual solutions

Fear is an emotion that affects our spirit, and some fears can only be stopped through spiritual means.

> *It is the spirit that quickeneth; the flesh profiteth nothing: the words that I speak unto you, they are spirit, and they are life.*
> JOHN 6:63

Jesus said His words are spirit and life. This implies that to fight a spiritual problem, you will need to apply the word of Jesus against it.

> *And David spake to the men that stood by him, saying, What shall be done to the man that killeth this Philistine, and taketh away the reproach from Israel? For who is this uncircumcised Philistine, that he should defy the armies of the living God?*
> 1 SAMUEL 17:26

In this verse, David declared that Goliath had defied the armies of the living God. The phrase "armies of the living God" was a quotation from the Word of God in Exodus 7:4: *But Pharaoh shall not hearken unto you, that I may lay my hand upon Egypt, and bring forth mine armies, and my people the children of Israel, out of the land of Egypt by great judgments.*

God said that Israel's armies are His armies. When David declared this word, he was directly releasing the power of God's Word against every contrary spirit that Goliath carried – particularly the spirit of fear.

Whenever you speak a word that comes from the mouth of God against your fear, you will bring that fear into subjection to the Word of God.

Therefore, to be able to stop your fear, search through the Bible for the right word from God that addresses your kind of fear.

For example, if the devil attacks your mind with the fear of death, you can always silence him using this verse:

> *I shall not die, but live, and declare the works of the LORD.*
> PSALM 118:17

If God has spoken that you will not die, why should you now believe a liar telling you that you will die?

Similarly, if the devil threatens your mind with a negative future, you can silence him with this verse:

> *For I know the thoughts that I think toward you, saith the LORD, thoughts of peace, and not of evil, to give you an expected end.*
> JEREMIAH 29:11

If God almighty has promised you peace and the attainment of your goals, why should you now trust a liar telling you a contrary outcome?

Fight a spirit with the Spirit. You can't silence a spirit of fear using human words and ideology, because it is only the Holy Spirit – at work in you – that can conquer evil spirits.

6. Speak to your fear

If the cause of fear is a spirit, it is able to hear your word when it is rooted in the Word of God.

> *Then said David to the Philistine, Thou comest to me with a sword, and with a spear, and with a shield: but I come to thee in the name of the LORD of hosts, the God of the armies of Israel, whom thou hast defied.* 1 SAMUEL 17:45

Here David spoke to Goliath, the fear of Israel. For every word from the mouth of Goliath, David released another word to neutralise and debunk it. Do not keep silent and allow your fear to speak lies into your mind and spirit. You will need to speak continually to your fear.

When your fear speaks words to frighten you, you will need to debunk it by speaking another word from the Bible to counter and silence it. Speak to your fear. When your fear tells you that you will die, tell your fear that you will not die but live. If your fear tells you that you will lose, tell your fear that you will not lose but gain. If your fear tells you that evil that happened to you in the past will happen to you again, tell your fear that affliction shall not occur the second time. Tell your fear that it is a liar and it should shut up.

Finally, it is noticed that in the conversation between David and Goliath, David spoke last. If your fear tells you that you will die ten times, reply to your fear at least eleven times that you will not die but live. Ensure you have the last word.

7. Speak to your fear in Jesus' name

> *Then said David to the Philistine, Thou comest to me with a sword, and with a spear, and with a shield: but I come to thee in the name of the LORD of hosts, the God of the armies of Israel, whom thou hast defied.* 1 SAMUEL 17:45

In this verse, David told Goliath that he had come against him in the name of God.

When you want to stop your fear, do it in Jesus' name. Fear is from the devil, and as a Christian, God has given you a name that is above every other name – the name of Jesus.

> *That at the name of Jesus every knee should bow, of things in heaven, and things in earth, and things under the earth; and that every tongue should confess that Jesus Christ is Lord, to the glory of God the Father.* PHILIPPIANS 2:10-11

The Word of God says that at the mention of the name of Jesus Christ; every tongue must confess that Jesus Christ is the Lord. When you speak to the spirit of fear in the name of Jesus Christ, it must surrender to the Lordship of Jesus in your situation. Jesus Christ is the Lord of your life; He is the one who will determine what to permit and what not to permit in your life. The devil and all his agents have no right to determine what happens to you.

Therefore, all their lies coming to your mind through the spirit of fear will go silent when they hear you speaking to them in the name of Jesus Christ.

So, when the spirit of fear tells you that you will have an accident, reply to it that you will not have an accident in the name of Jesus Christ. Expose and defeat all its lies in the name of Jesus Christ.

8. Stick to your conviction

> *David said moreover, The LORD that delivered me out of the paw of the lion, and out of the paw of the bear, he will deliver me out of the hand of this Philistine. And Saul said unto David, Go, and the LORD be with thee.* 1 SAMUEL 17:37

Before David said this, Saul had warned David that he couldn't fight Goliath because of his lack of experience. Fear of man is a spirit and it is from the devil. When the devil can't speak to your mind directly through the spirit of fear, he can speak into your mind using the mouth of human vessels he has captured. The spirit of Goliath had captured Saul. Saul was the greatest warrior of the Israelites and yet even he was afraid of Goliath. Therefore, that spirit was able to speak to David through Saul.

Similarly, the spirit of fear can speak to your mind using the mouths of people around you, especially those that you have special respect for. Such people could be your spouse or a close associate. When the devil begins to speak fear into your mind through people around you, let those people know your conviction as David did to Saul. If they tell you that your fear is real, let them know that you don't accept that because; God is with you.

When people tell you that your sickness is incurable because experts have said so, tell them that you disagree with them on the basis of the Word of God. Stick to your biblical conviction.

9. Do not reason with the devil

> *And Saul said to David, Thou art not able to go against this Philistine to fight with him: for thou art but a youth, and he a man of war from his youth.* 1 SAMUEL 17:33

In this verse, Saul was trying to call David to his senses by explaining the reason for his belief that David would not be able to defeat Goliath. He was trying to show David the situation from a human perspective, mentioning factors such as experience and age. But David refused to be limited to human wisdom.

> *David said moreover, The LORD that delivered me out of the paw of the lion, and out of the paw of the bear, he will deliver me out of the hand of this Philistine. And Saul said unto David, Go, and the LORD be with thee.* 1 SAMUEL 17:37

When Saul discovered that David was not giving in to Saul's rational argument, he let him go. You must be aware that the spirit of fear will always try to be logical when speaking to your mind, coming across as reasonable and rational. You have to decide that you will not listen to the devil, no matter how sensible his persuasions seem. It is all cleverly cooked-up lies. Moreover, the Word of God is never limited to human understanding, and often appears to contradict it. Do not try to rationalise the Word of God in regard to your situation, because it may not appear logical.

10. Check for good news

Fear is all about bad news and bad events.

> *David said moreover, The LORD that delivered me out of the paw of the lion, and out of the paw of the bear, he will deliver me out of the hand of this Philistine. And Saul said unto David, Go, and the LORD be with thee.* 1 SAMUEL 17:37

After a series of negative statements from Saul, David declared good news to counteract Saul's lack of faith and silence him. While Saul was focusing on Goliath's strengths, David chose to remember the good news of his past achievements with God's strength. He told Saul how God gave him victory against dangerous animals in the desert. The good news silences the bad news.

Fear is all about potential bad news. If you thoroughly examine all the things making you afraid, you will discover that they are all about bad news. Therefore, to stop the flow of bad news that the enemy has prepared to keep you under fear, speak out good news. The Word of God is good news! All the goodness of God you have enjoyed are good news. All the promises of God to us are good news. You have a lot of good news to declare to silence your enemy.

So when the devil raises people up to speak potential bad news into your mind, reply with good news. Let them know that your God is good and He is always doing you good, and that He will continue to do you good. Stop your fear with good news.

11. God is already against your fear

> *This day will the LORD deliver thee into mine hand; and I will smite thee, and take thine head from thee; and I will give the carcases of the host of the Philistines this day unto the fowls of the air, and to the wild beasts of the earth; that all the earth may know that there is a God in Israel.* 1 SAMUEL 17:46

David told Goliath that God would deliver him into his hand, that God will work against Goliath to make him fall. Truly, God is always against whatever evil comes against you. Your God is against the spirit of fear that comes against your peace. The Lord is already against the anxiety troubling your heart. God is already against every spirit hindering your faith in Him. In every negative situation that you find yourself in, your God is already against it. Whatever the devil brings to frighten you is already under the attack of your God.

> *For thus saith the LORD of hosts; After the glory hath he sent me unto the nations which spoiled you: for he that toucheth you toucheth the apple of his eye.* ZECHARIAH 2:8

It is the promise of God that whatever comes against you also comes against your God, so there is no contest. Therefore, even if what you are afraid of eventually materialises, it will suffer serious attack from your God. So whatever the possible outcome of the threat that fear is bringing into your mind, you will still win in the end. Therefore, there is no reason to fear.

12. Keep the passion

Fear is all about bad news and this weighs down the heart. You will need to be resolute and maintain your passion as you come against your fear.

> *And it came to pass, when the Philistine arose, and came, and drew nigh to meet David, that David hastened, and ran toward the army to meet the Philistine.* 1 SAMUEL 17:48

David ran into battle against Goliath. He was so excited to face Goliath; he did not face Goliath crying. You don't face your fears by begging or weeping but by being active when confronting them. For example, if you are going to demand your rights from an oppressive manager, you have to show passion, boldness and be active. If you are shy and lack confidence, looking downwards, he or she will not take you seriously. Lift up your head and confront situations boldly in order to stop them from continuing to attack you!

13. Avoid being natural

> *And David girded his sword upon his armour, and he assayed to go; for he had not proved it. And David said unto Saul, I cannot*

> *go with these; for I have not proved them. And David put them off him.* 1 SAMUEL 17:39

Saul was thinking naturally in his ideas about how to stop Goliath. He gave his armour to David to face Goliath, but David refused it. As long as you remain natural in your thinking and imagination, the spirit of fear will succeed in convincing you about its so-called dangers. You will need to operate in the supernatural in order to silence your fear.

For example, it may be natural to experience a certain discomfort if you have a disease, and the more you yield to this natural occurrence; the more you will make yourself easy prey to the spirit of fear. It will present you with further negative possibilities. To silence the spirit of fear, you will need to refuse to be natural, as it wants to take you through natural thinking that will eventually make you afraid.

To defeat the many lies of the devil, you have to believe in God's intervention and expect miracles in your situation. Therefore, if the devil attacks you with fear by telling you what normally happens in your situation, you can overcome him by telling him that God is in the business of miracles. If the devil tries to frighten you by reminding you of your lack of resources, let him know that your God is a miraculous provider.

14. Get rid of everything that speaks fear to you

In order to perpetuate its work of threats, a spirit of fear might have established certain channels around you through which it communicates fear to you. In order to stop fear, you will need to identify all these channels and get rid of them. When you remove all the structures, it is exploiting to communicate fear to you, you will make it difficult for the spirit of fear to maintain its delivery of threats to your mind.

> *And David said to Saul, Let no man's heart fail because of him; thy servant will go and fight with this Philistine.* 1 SAMUEL 17:32

In this verse, David sent a message to Israel's soldiers that they no longer needed to fear Goliath. Even before David went into battle, he was predicting victory. In doing so, he was encouraging the army and so cutting off any channel the devil may have exploited to spread fear to David. If a shepherd like David wasn't afraid, why did the experienced soldiers of Israel need to be afraid? If they began to think like that, they wouldn't undermine David's confidence by warning him of this, that and the other as he approached the battle.

In order to stop the fear in your life, you will need to avoid the people the devil is using to speak fear into your mind. Similarly, you will need to get rid of any structure or system around your life; that communicates fear to you. Such structures could be an image, music or things that keep alive the memory of your bitter past experience. Close down all these channels of fear around your life.

15. There is another possibility

Fear speaks about negative possibilities but faith speaks about positive possibilities. Fear proclaims possible evil outcomes but faith proclaims possible favourable outcomes.

> *And the Philistine said to David, Come to me, and I will give thy flesh unto the fowls of the air, and to the beasts of the field.* 1 SAMUEL 17:44

Here Goliath proclaimed the evil outcome that he wanted for David. He was trying to speak fear into David's heart.

> *This day will the LORD deliver thee into mine hand; and I will smite thee, and take thine head from thee; and I will give the*

> *carcases of the host of the Philistines this day unto the fowls of the air, and to the wild beasts of the earth; that all the earth may know that there is a God in Israel.* 1 SAMUEL 17:46

David counteracted Goliath's negativity with words about the favourable outcome he believed God would give him. Both fear and faith focus on the possible outcomes; while fear is negative, faith is positive. At the end of this scenario, the faith of David defeated the fear of Goliath.

> *Now faith is the substance of things hoped for, the evidence of things not seen.* HEBREWS 11:1

Faith is about expecting a favourable outcome. Faith conquers fear and whenever fear comes to you, you must reply to it with faith. When the voice of fear speaks into your mind, you must speak back with the voice of faith.

There are many places in the Bible where the people of God responded with faith when the enemy exploited their difficult situation to speak fear into their minds. With their word of faith, they were able to stop and conquer their fears.

> *Above all, taking the shield of faith, wherewith ye shall be able to quench all the fiery darts of the wicked.* EPHESIANS 6:16

One of the fiery darts of the wicked is the arrow of fear. It is only through the demonstration of faith that you can extinguish such an evil arrow.

For example, Caleb withstood the fears of the other spies when they came back to the Israelites and reported that the land of Canaan was too strong to be taken. He spoke in faith: *"Let us go up at once, and possess it; for we are well able to overcome it"* (Numbers

13:30). Unfortunately, most of the other spies gave in to their fears and the people believed their negative reports.

If God is for you, then, no one can stand against you. Do not be afraid of many enemies, for your God is stronger than all of them.

> *For I know that my redeemer liveth, and that he shall stand at the latter day upon the earth…* JOB 19:25

In his terrible situation and facing mockery from close friends, Job chose to maintain his faith in God by incessantly confessing the truth about God. While Job did not know why his terrible troubles had come upon him, he continued to believe that God was his redeemer. That is faith. While you may not be able to answer many questions about your challenges in life, at least; you can stand on the fact that your God lives and He is on your side. That is faith.

> *If it be so, our God whom we serve is able to deliver us from the burning fiery furnace, and he will deliver us out of thine hand, O king.* DANIEL 3:17

The three Hebrews who said this were confronted with the fire of the enemy in a foreign land, but they refused to surrender to fear. They chose to keep putting their trust in God. That did not stop the enemy from throwing them into the fire, yet, even then the three men maintained their confidence in their God and their God came through for them.

As Job discovered, there is little point in asking God why He allows certain ugly situations in your life, as often, we are not given the reasons. But if we can stick to our faith in Him, whatever the circumstances, then like Job and the three Hebrews in the fire, we will experience His deliverance in the long run, whatever we have to go through in the meantime.

Don't let the enemy make you doubt God, even when He allows a series of challenges to come your way. Keep the faith, and you shall see your fear no more.

> *Now when Daniel knew that the writing was signed, he went into his house; and his windows being open in his chamber toward Jerusalem, he kneeled upon his knees three times a day, and prayed, and gave thanks before his God, as he did aforetime.*
> DANIEL 6:10

After Daniel's enemies had succeeded in manipulating the king to order a decree of death in order to trap Daniel, Daniel refused to focus on the threat but on his God. All the attempts of his enemies to stop him from serving his God failed. Because Daniel refused to renounce his God, his God came through for him. If you can refuse to doubt your God, which fear tries to make you do, then your God will come through for you.

JUST ONE STONE

> *And David put his hand in his bag, and took thence a stone, and slang it, and smote the Philistine in his forehead, that the stone sunk into his forehead; and he fell upon his face to the earth.*
> 1 SAMUEL 17:49

In the end, David stopped Goliath with just one stone. To stop Goliath did not need Saul's armour and neither did it need better experience, as Saul thought. It did not even need many people, for it was only David that God used to remove the uncircumcised Philistine from the way of Israel.

Faith is the greatest stopper. Faith can stop any fear and it can quench any flaming arrow the enemy may throw at your mind. If David could stop Goliath using an ordinary stone, you can do the same to your 'giant' if you exercise the same faith.

Do not let fear tear you into pieces, arise and stop it now. Do not let fear keep you in a mental prison, arise and stop it now. Do not let fear demobilise you, arise and stop it now. With God on your side, you don't need anything big to conquer your fear, for your God is bigger than the mightiest. It was just an ordinary stone that brought mighty Goliath down. The battle against fear can't be won through human strategies but through our spiritual weapons that never fail.

> *For the weapons of our warfare are not carnal, but mighty through God to the pulling down of strong holds;) casting down imaginations, and every high thing that exalteth itself against the knowledge of God, and bringing into captivity every thought to the obedience of Christ; and having in a readiness to revenge all disobedience, when your obedience is fulfilled.*
> 2 CORINTHIANS 10:4-6

Chapter 6

FEAR NOT

'Fear ye not therefore, ye are of more value than many sparrows.'
MATTHEW 10:31

Jesus told his disciples not to be afraid. As you are also one of His disciples, Jesus is telling you the same. There are several reasons why you should not fear, which include the following:

1. There will be supply in famine

> *And Elijah said unto her, Fear not; go and do as thou hast said: but make me therefore a little cake first, and bring it unto me, and after make for thee and for thy son. For thus saith the LORD God of Israel, The barrel of meal shall not waste, neither shall the cruse of oil fail, until the day that the LORD sendeth rain upon the earth.* 1 KINGS 17:13-14

In the midst of famine, God remembered a poor widow. That God is still alive and He is still in the business of supplying the needs of those who have needs. Fear not, because God will supply all your needs according to His riches in glory.

2. There are blessings in the journey of life

Something good is awaiting you in the future, so don't be afraid of the future.

> *And there is hope in thine end, saith the LORD, that thy children shall come again to their own border.* JEREMIAH 31:17

Because God has promised that; there is hope in the future, there are blessings in your tomorrow.

> *And the LORD appeared unto him the same night, and said, I am the God of Abraham thy father: fear not, for I am with thee, and will bless thee, and multiply thy seed for my servant Abraham's sake.* GENESIS 26:24

All Christians are Abraham's spiritual descendants. The promises of God to Abraham apply to us, as we have been grafted into the tree of Israel (see Romans 11:17). God promised a future to Abraham, and so we partake of that future too. Don't be afraid of your future because it will be glorious.

3. There shall be strength in weakness

God promises that your weakness will not limit you because He will supply strength when you need it. So don't be afraid of your limitations. Isaiah 41:10 guarantees God's strength for us: *"Fear thou not; for I am with thee: be not dismayed; for I am thy God: I will strengthen thee; yea, I will help thee; yea, I will uphold thee with the right hand of my righteousness."*

You can now say with boldness: *"I can do all things through Christ which strengtheneth me"* (Philippians 4:13).

4. There is companionship in trial

Don't be afraid of tests because you will never be alone. God will always be with you in all your trials.

Isaiah 43:1-2 says: *"But now thus saith the LORD that created thee, O Jacob, and he that formed thee, O Israel, Fear not: for I have redeemed thee, I have called thee by thy name; thou art mine. When thou passest through the waters, I will be with thee; and through the rivers, they shall not overflow thee: when thou walkest through the fire, thou shalt not be burned; neither shall the flame kindle upon thee."*

The holy one of Israel is giving you a promise that He will always be with you in all your confrontations, so don't be afraid of the tests and trials of life. No challenge shall overpower you because the God who is greater than the greatest will always be with you.

5. There shall be protection in danger

Fear no evil, because you will see it and hear about it but it shall not come to you. God has provided adequate security for you in the journey of life.

Psalm 91:7-10 gives the assurance that *"a thousand shall fall at thy side, and ten thousand at thy right hand; but it shall not come nigh thee. Only with thine eyes shalt thou behold and see the reward of the wicked. Because thou hast made the LORD, which is my refuge, even the most High, thy habitation; there shall no evil befall thee, neither shall any plague come nigh thy dwelling."*

God has provided divine immunity for you. You are immune against every evil of the world.

6. There is overshadowing care for you

You don't need to be afraid for your survival.

> *But the very hairs of your head are all numbered. Fear ye not therefore, ye are of more value than many sparrows.* MATTHEW 10:30-31

The value of an article determines the level of care from the owner. You are precious in the eyes of the Lord, so, He cares about your survival. God has made provision for your care; fear not. Due to your value, God is not ready to allow the enemy to mess you up. God wants you, that is why He created you.

7. There is life beyond the grave

Do not be afraid of death; it is not the end but the beginning of a better experience. Resist every attempt of the enemy to threaten you with death.

> *And when I saw him, I fell at his feet as dead. And he laid his right hand upon me, saying unto me, Fear not; I am the first and the last: I am he that liveth, and was dead; and, behold, I am alive for evermore, Amen; and have the keys of hell and of death.*
> REVELATION 1:17-18

The keys of hell and death are in the hands of your God, not the devil. It is your God who will determine who in God's kingdom should die and who should live. When the devil threatens you with the fear of death, resist him; you can't die until God wants you home. Take more risks (but not stupid ones!), try new things – nothing can kill you until your time is up. Don't be stagnant because of the fear of death. Try new ideas. Fear not.

8. There is a divine presence around you

> *When thou goest out to battle against thine enemies, and seest horses, and chariots, and a people more than thou, be not afraid of them: for the LORD thy God is with thee, which brought thee up out of the land of Egypt.* DEUTERONOMY 20:1

God promised Israel not to be afraid of many enemies coming against them, for His divine presence was always with them to defend them. No matter how strong and how many your enemies may be, your God is far stronger than them. Fear not.

9. There shall be a way

> *Behold, I will do a new thing; now it shall spring forth; shall ye not know it? I will even make a way in the wilderness, and rivers in the desert.* ISAIAH 43:19

God promised Israel that He would make a way for them. Which kind of way are you seeking for? Is it a way of escape from danger? God shall make a way for you. Is it a way of promotion? God shall make a way for you. Fear not; for God shall make a way.

10. There shall be termination of your troublers

> *And Moses said unto the people, Fear ye not, stand still, and see the salvation of the LORD, which he will shew to you to day: for the Egyptians whom ye have seen to day, ye shall see them again no more for ever.* EXODUS 14:13

Moses prophesied to Israel that; they would see their troublers no more, and it came true. Is someone troubling you and causing you fear? Fear not, for you shall see them no more. Just wait for the salvation of the Lord in your situation and you will testify to His deliverance.

11. There shall be no defeat

> *What shall we then say to these things? If God be for us, who can be against us?* ROMANS 8:31

God is for you. God is with you. God is inside of you. God will work for you, work with you and work through you. Fear not, for greater is He that is in you; than the one in the world. With God on your side, victory is assured.

12. There shall be no fulfilment of the enemy's word

> *Take counsel together, and it shall come to nought; speak the word, and it shall not stand: for God is with us.* ISAIAH 8:10

No evil word you hear will be fulfilled. This is because it is only the counsel for your God that shall be established. Fear not the evil word of your enemy; it shall not come to pass.

BOOKS FROM THE SAME AUTHOR

Journey to the Next Level

The New Creature

Building a Glorious Home: A Pathway to Successful Marriage

The Enemy of Marriage

Words That Heal

The Winning Formula

Faith That Always Wins

Common Mistakes Parents Make About Their Children

Recovery is Possible

When You Are Desperate for a Miracle

Decision (Explore the Path to Wise Decision-Making)

I Refuse to be Deceived

This book and all other books from the same author are available at Christian bookstores and distributors worldwide.

They can also be obtained through online retail partners such as Amazon or by contacting the author at the address below:

Pastor Fatai Kasali
21-23 Stokescroft
Bristol
BS1 3PY
UK

Telephone: 00447727159581
E-mail: info@fkasali.com
Website: www.fkasali.com

www.ingramcontent.com/pod-product-compliance
Lightning Source LLC
Chambersburg PA
CBHW050042080526
44586CB00014B/1411